GUS JOSEPH

Don't Find Time. Create It.

Philosophies and practices to make your time more effective.

Contents

1

Introduction

What do Elon Musk, Queen Elizabeth and Christiano Ronaldo all have in common? The same thing that the College student, the McDonalds employee and hunter from the African tribe do. It's the same thing your Dad, Mum and even YOU have in common. It is TIME. We all have 24 hours in a day. So, how do we all share this valuable resource, yet live very different lives?

Time is the greatest resource we have. This book will share philosophies and practices on how we can best utilize this gift to get the most out of our days and live a fruitful life. By respecting our time, we can maximize our productivity so we can gain the freedom to do the things that we want to do. This will increase our energy and shape us to think in a way that can maximize us living the human experience. Let's face it, we're all going to die one day. So, why not utilize the time that we have here to live life on our terms. We have this blessing and we must respect it. This book will provide the philosophies and thought processes in how we can best think about our time. It will also give practices we can do daily in ensuring that we can use our time most effectively. With that being said, let's not waste any time and jump right into it! I will show you how to create time for you to live your best life, enjoy and get more done!

2

Mindset

It is important to take the actions everyday that will contribute to our best long-term future. It can be easy to give into our emotions. Perhaps we want to hit that snooze button or don't feel like working out. What would your future self think about these actions? What would your ancestors who faced plagues and world wars think about you not wanting to get out of bed? Feelings are great. It's a part of the human experience. However, our feelings can hold us back from living our truly best lives. You may think to yourself "I can start tomorrow" or "I'll begin focusing on this new goal on January 1st". That right there is a losing mentality. It takes a long time to develop new habits and replace the old ones. Those habits are often instilled from the environment we grew up in and the people who were around us. They have influenced our day to day living and actions. This comes back to how we value and spend our time.

The greatest use of our time is in our self-education. The areas I deem as most valuable are in health, wealth, relationships and higher purpose. Being educated in your health and living by a standard where you value this attribute and maintain it daily will put you in a position where you have more energy and can enjoy your time that you have here. Understanding wealth and how to best accumulate it while being disciplined gives you more freedom with your time. Money is merely a tool that gives you the freedom to do the things you want when you want to do them. Your relationship with yourself is the most important. You are with yourself every single day. No one knows you better than you know yourself. You know your talents, fears and what you are naturally drawn towards. Getting to truly know yourself must be our priority so we don't waste time pursuing things we don't really want to do to please people we may not even like. If we best know ourselves, we can communicate who we are to other people in our lives. We can find like-minded individuals who challenge us to be the best version of ourselves. These are the types of people who are willing to have tough conversations with us because they genuinely care about us. They also can celebrate our victories with us. By best knowing who we are and communicating that to others in an authentic way is how we can best attract these types of people into our lives. The final sector is higher purpose. Some people know exactly what this higher purpose is in their younger years. Perhaps they want to be a musician, doctor or a Pokemon trainer. Maybe these pathways change or they continue on. For the rest of us who are still unsure, we get closer to figuring it out by continuing to develop ourselves. This is through the pursuit of education and life experiences. This shapes our character and we get to better know who we are and what we really care about.

The sooner you can understand the fundamentals and importance of health, wealth, relationships and higher purpose, the sooner you can live life to your absolute fullest. This allows us to make the most of the time that we have in this world. We will be diving deeper into these areas of importance.

3

Health

This is what gives us the vitality and energy to truly live life. When we are healthy physically, mentally and spiritually, we are in alignment. It helps us live a quality life and enjoy the things that we want to spend our time doing.

Psychical health is how we take care of our bodies. Are we putting clean foods into our body? Are we exercising in the form of cardio and resistance training? Are we getting adequate sleep? These are all vital for our physical health. I promise you this. You will never regret a workout in your life. You may feel apprehensive towards it at the beginning. However, once that workout is done, you will be met with the feeling of empowerment and euphoria. You will also have more of a presence of a champion. People who often workout walk around in a way where they are more confident and in tune with their bodies. Also, it is a great self-confidence builder to see your body literally transform. As you workout more often, you will notice how much more effective you are with your time. You will feel more energized in your body and some tasks that would drain your time and energy will feel easier if you have this area handled. The internet is a great resource to help you better learn more about the physical benefits of working out as well as what exercise routine may be best for you.

Mental health is defined as a person's condition in regards to their psychological and emotional wellbeing. Having a healthy mental health allows us to feel and operate at our best. When we take care of both our psychological and emotional needs, we are able to best utilize our time and act effectively. It allows us to also enjoy our time better in our lives. We can best take care of our mental health by taking time to prioritize the things that matter the most to our long-term goals while making sure we are taking care of our psychological and emotional wellbeing. Some practices daily to take care of our mental health can be things such as journaling, affirming things we're grateful for and checking in with ourselves to make sure we are living in alignment with our values and goals we are working towards. If there are things that we have which we need to heal from, we can acknowledge them and find the necessary assistance to heal them. When we have these things in order, we are less distracted and more aligned with how we can use our time to push towards our goals.

Spiritual health can be defined as what is the greater good. I personally believe that the greatest gift you can give to the universe is your own personal transformation. That is why it is on us to be the best versions we can be. To be the best version of yourself is to be who you truly are at your core. We have a mission while we are here find out who we are. We do this through life experience, education and being open to other people's viewpoints of reality. Ultimately, we must create win/win scenarios for those that we meet in our lives. If both people are winning, then that create a more positive and prosperous future for all. It's on all of us to define what spiritual or philosophical path that may be. These can be based off guiding values often given to us through our upbringing or influences. It is on us to find what really matters. The sooner we find this, the sooner we can unlock our full potential and a life that is worthwhile. When we figure this out, this can translate to finding ways to build wealth or a career of purpose and passion that can give us riches.

4

Wealth

True freedom is to be able to do the things we want to do when we want to do them. There is no greater path to freedom than that of financial freedom. With this, you are able to access the healthiest foods, travel anywhere you would want to go in the world and take care of the people that you love. Some people are born knowing what they want to do exactly. They may want to be a musician, doctor or superhero. Sometimes these dream career paths can make a lot of sense, and sometimes they are less reliable. If you are unsure of the exact career path of what you enjoy and can be compensated for, I'd suggest trying a wide variety of careers to find what really sticks out to you. You may do something that you love, but it may not pay you what you desire. If it has the potential to do so, it may be a good long-term investment. In the current internet marketplace, it provides more flexibility to do what you actually want to do. You are able to make a living from sharing your passion online.

The greatest way to build wealth is by educating yourself. Understand what an asset and liability are. Become as valuable as you can to the workforce through skills, experience and always going above and beyond. If you are reading a book like this, you are already on the right track. Understand how to save money while investing it appropriately in real estate, stocks, crypto and your own education especially. When you are going to school or work on a regular 9-5 cycle Monday-Friday, begin prioritizing the time you are off to learn more about the accumulation of wealth. When you are young and especially if you take care of your health, you will have more energy to put into this. This education will compound over time. I recommend looking things up on the internet and Youtube to better understand how to build wealth habits. You can definitely maximize your time through your wealth education by simple habits such as listening to podcast, audiobooks and lectures about wealth accumulation during your commute, workout or home chores. When we exchange money, it is a value exchange. People pay one another because it solves a pain point or gives pleasure to someone. This can be in the form of buying products or services from people. We get our money from other people if they see value in what we have to offer. That is why it is important to keep up with these relationships that we build throughout our lives.

5

Relationships

Our relationships can help us save time drastically when we are trying to learn or accomplish our goals. Our experiences in life are more fulfilling when we share it with those we love. When we can create win/win scenarios in our relationships, we can better leverage our time and resource to operate most effectively. This can be in the simple example of growing up in a home with siblings. Everyone may be given a task to do that needs to be done before dinner is served. Perhaps you have or had housemates at one point. It was more effective when you could work together and delegate tasks so you could spend more time doing the things you wanted to do.

A smart man learns from their own mistakes, while a wise man learns from the mistakes of others. There's no greater teacher than life itself. However, there are some things that we can learn from others without having to make the mistakes ourselves. Tell people you care about what you're working on. They may be able to get you there faster than if you were to go alone. You may even have goals that align with this person. Maybe they are wanting to get more in shape and you are also. You can use this to hold each other accountable while encouraging one another's goals. You also get to build a special bond and celebrate your wins together. This is one of the greatest joys of the human experience.

If you have a goal that you are working towards, be sure to set healthy boundaries with those you care about. You may be pursuing a business that you can build after work. This could be the usual time that you spend with your partner. Be sure to communicate to them how important this goal is to you. Many top athletes and professionals are faced with the tough decision of pursuing their craft at the highest level or going to that get together. You may have to miss some of those events in order to pursue your goals that are important to your future self. If they love you, they will understand. Be sure to tell them in a confident and loving way. Then, when you do spend time with them you can make the time as top quality as possible. Finding what is most important to you comes from finding what your higher purpose is.

6

Higher purpose

A great tool for figuring this out is to look at the 'Ikigai'. This is a Japanese concept referring to something that gives an individual a sense of purpose, reason for living, what the world needs and something that can pay well. Below is a snapshot example of an Ikigai.

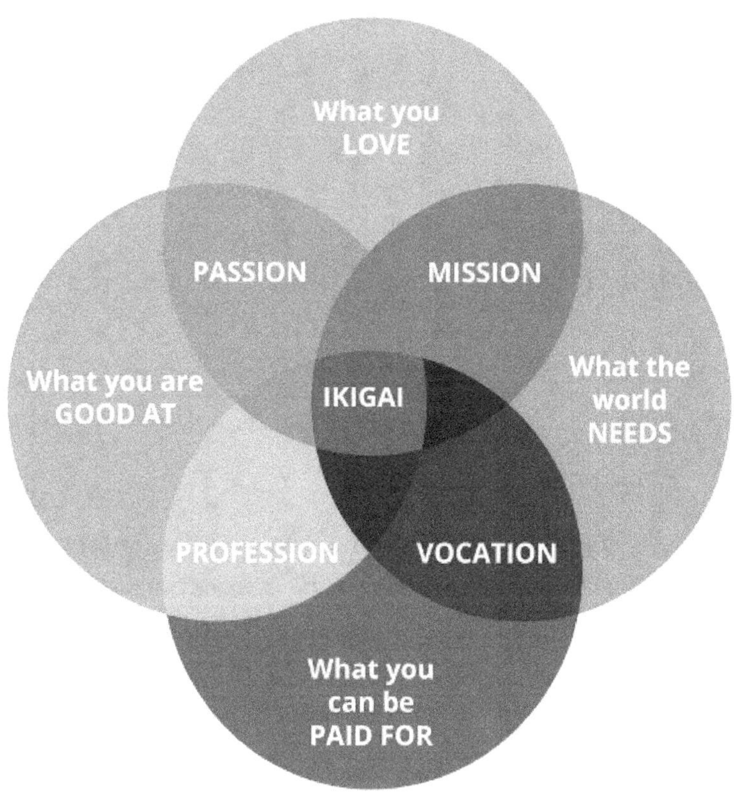

Work on this at least once a year deeply as there is a good chance that it can change over time. As you experience more in life, you begin to understand who you are more at a core level. When you have done the work on your health, wealth and relationships, the higher purpose will start to become clearer to you.

7

Get up earlier

Do you ever feel like you don't have enough time for yourself? You have commitments to work, schooling or other people in the morning. Perhaps you have children or family members who need your attention. Are you struggling to find the time? I have a solution for you. Simply, you must create the time. We can't actually create more than 24 hours in a day. However, we can get up an hour earlier. That's a whole hour of time just for you in the morning. I'm not saying to neglect your sleep. Sleep is extremely important. What I am saying is to be really honest with yourself. Are you laying in bed after you wake up? Or are you springing straight into action? Are you rolling over to get to your phone and do you hit snooze? Perhaps you begin checking your emails and texts in the morning upon getting up. What about you? Where is your time? If you don't have time for your own life. You don't have a life. Someone else owns it.

So how then can we reclaim this sacred time of ours? It's simple. Get up earlier and make sure it is your time. This has become more difficult in the technology era. Technology has become the biggest distractor for us. We don't prioritize time for ourselves. That hour of time we gain by getting up earlier can contribute drastically to our wellbeing and life goals. Perhaps you've set yourself a health and fitness goal. There's no better time to work towards that than in the morning. It's one of the best ways to start your day. It may seem tiring when you first begin using this new found time to workout. However, you begin to gain more energy when you do it consistently. Have you ever noticed that people who tend to exercise have a certain energy level to them? Generally, they have higher energy levels. Especially if they do this in the morning. When you commit to working out in the morning, you have already conquered a huge feat when people are just beginning to get out of bed. This may be something simple like walking around your neighborhood or joining your local workout class. From my personal life, I have never once regretted working out after 6+ years of doing so. It is something that builds your energy level, fitness, strength and character.

8

Set timers

Timers can be one of the most useful tools when it comes to doing deep work. Having a schedule gives us structure. Timers are a useful tool for accomplishing tasks throughout the day. This is especially applicable when you need to engage in deep work. Start off small when beginning deep work with pure focus. I'd suggest setting a timer for 20 minutes of pure focus towards the task at hand that you are doing. Even if we go to work at a 9-5 or are in school right now, we are not using that full time to engage in deep work on a daily basis. Let's be really honest with ourselves here. We are usually in auto pilot mode or we may have distractions that come up like other people or our social media.

Often, we can fall into the trap of mismanaging our time as we believe we have more time than we thought we did. Perhaps you have an assignment that is due in two weeks. You think to yourself "I have plenty of time to get that done. I'll do it later". It then ends up creeping up on you and then it gets done last minute at a subpar level. This psychological phenomenon is known as Parkinson's Law. This is defined as when you have something that must be done with a given deadline but rather than doing it straight away, you stretch out the time of when you do it. You end up doing it towards the tail-end of your deadline. Can you think of times in your life when you have fallen into this trap? That's ok. This is more common than you think it is. You may think in your mind that it makes sense to put something off and do it at a later date. When you do this, you have no idea what emergency or other priority may come up towards your deadline of the task you had planned to do later. Also, the task at hand remains in your mind during this whole time. So, it ends up taking up more time than you thought it did. This is why timers can be a great tool for making sure you get these tasks completed in a timely manner while allowing scheduled breaks for yourself.

9

Remove distractions

We have been blessed by technology. We have the ability to access any information we could have never imagined before. This is all at our finger tips. We have the ability to connect with those who are closet to us via social media and are provided by endless entertainment through our phones and other screen related items. However, this has also made it extremely difficult to focus deeply on something that we are wanting to do. When was the last time you checked your screen time? It will surprise you how often we use our phones on a daily basis. I'd encourage you to set yourself a goal of having your weekly screen time amount use to go down by 20% in the next week.

How can we best remove these distractions? There's a few simple ways in doing this. Turn your phone off. When was the last time you shut your phone off? When your phone is off, it is less distracting. It takes time to turn your phone back on, and by that time you may decide against turning it on. If that is too extreme for you, then consider placing your phone in a different room or in your backpack. Just that extra steps required to access your phone can make all the difference of you realizing what you're doing. When we have an instinctual habit of reaching for our phones which are usually right there, we access it without even thinking. Perhaps you need to have your phone on you in case of an emergency. You can setup your phone so that certain people such as immediate family can access you while it's on sleep mode with everyone else unable to do so. Most of the time when someone is reaching out, you don't need to see what they reached out to you about straight away. If it's really important, they will call you multiple times. You can setup your phone so that when someone calls you twice in a row, it will notify you.

My final tip is to use the grayscale method. Grayscale turns your phone into a black and white mode. We get stimulated by colors and these social media sites and phones games understand this about our psychology. Grayscale make the phone less stimulating and honestly stale. However, it allows you to access and function your phone just as you would always do so. You just don't have color. This personally has been proven to be effective for myself and friends I have told about it. I found myself naturally using my phone less.

-In order to do this on the iPhone:
   1) you must go to your settings.
   2) Then go to Accessibility.
   3) Click on the Display & Text Size tab.
   4) Scroll down to Color Filters.
   5) Turn on that setting and then select Grayscale.

As the name implies, it makes everything look gray. You won't notice it at first in terms of your time spent on your phone. However, you will naturally end up using your phone less. Most likely, if you're not using an iPhone, there will be something similar you can use for your phone.

Google is you friend. Also, if you're really wanting to cut down with your screen time and other distractions, you can always revert back to a flip phone or older technology that can be used strictly only for phone calls. Set yourself up for success!

10

Educate while commuting

Technology is incredible. The ability we have with audio to consume content is amazing. There are a wide variety of resources we have online to educate ourselves. These include audio books on audible, podcasts and lectures. We also have the ability to speed up to a faster rate such as 1.5x speed. This allows us to consume education at a faster rate. Rather than listening to music, I'd encourage you to listen to more educational content. You can do this in the car on your commute, while you're doing chores around your home or while you're working out. This knowledge you consume will compound over time and you will have better tools for success or a better understanding of something you are excited to learn about.

11

Outsource your tasks

There is a value to your time. Depending on your current marketplace value, it can be wise to outsource your tasks to other people. Let's say, you have a career right now where you are earning $100,000 a year. That's roughly you being worth $50 per hour. You may need to clean your home. It may take you three hours to do that. That's roughly $150 of your time just to do that. Instead, you could hire someone for $30 an hour and it would take two hours. Your opportunity cost of you doing your own cleaning would cost you more than just hiring someone to clean your home. When you start to look at things in this way, you begin to use your time more proactively. Perhaps you may not be at that level of income yet. It may be worth it then to do certain tasks yourself. However, if these tasks end up being a whole day ordeal, it may make more sense to hire someone to help you with the particular task at hand.

Does Jeff Bezos pack, ship, handle customer calls and deliver your package to you when you order something on Amazon? No, he doesn't. He instead has created systems which allow Amazon to do all of these things. He has a huge team of people who contribute to making the delivery process as smooth as he can. Any business owner starts off doing things themselves when starting out. As they begin to see success in their business, they realize that they can be more productive when they begin outsourcing certain tasks that would be best delegated elsewhere. This allows them to focus on the grander vision and focus on the things that they do best while growing their businesses. Income tends to go up during this growth phase which allows for more people to be hired. Outsourcing your tasks is the key to maximizing your time and getting the best return on your most valuable resource.

12

Write down your goals with clear deadlines

There have been many studies correlated with writing down your goals and the levels of success achieved by people who do this action. However, there is an art to writing down your goals. For example, if you have a financial goal, it is more effective to be as precise as possible. If your goal is "I want to be richer". I can give you a dollar bill and you will indeed be richer. The goal has been achieved. Instead, if you had a goal more precise such as "In 10 years from now, I will be a millionaire. I will do this attracting high ticket clients through my sales job and investing a large portion of my income in the stock market via dollar cost averaging. I will increase my income on average by 15% per year through educating myself on how to be a better sales person through attending seminars, reading books and surrounding myself around other high performing individuals. I will read this every morning and night while tracking my progress once a month". This is a much more specific example than the first one we used. This second example is more likely to be followed as we have established s specific time measure, actions and a battle plan that we can follow to achieve our goals.

13

ABCDE Lists

We just spoke about goal setting. The next segment is what I call task setting. This is for things that are due on a daily of weekly basis. ABCDE list are great for helping us prioritize what is most important for us to get done. Below is an example of an ABCDE list:

A

- Get back to work email
- Enroll in classes for next school semester which open at 11am
- Double check before submitting assignment due at midnight tonight

B

- Get started on accounting homework due in 5 days
- Crush an epic leg day gym workout
- Meal prep for the week

C

- Put away dishes from dishwasher
- Do laundry
- Start listening to new podcast friend recommended

D

- Call friend back and catchup
- Take dog to dog park
- Re-watch lecture to take notes

E

- Wash couch cushions
- Go to CVS to print photos
- Look up recipes for healthy juice blends

As you can see from above, this is a structure with the core focus to help you best understand what to prioritize. The example ABCDE list I gave above may even have the exact same things for you but they may be in under a different letter. Plan on putting the most important tasks in the A section and have it vary from the first letters of top priority to the E section (low priority). The list can also change daily. Perhaps you have laundry that you need to get done, but you don't need to do it for a few days. It may be a C level task. However, you may not get to it as you are focused on other tasks you are doing. After three days, you may run out of clothing and this could end up becoming an A task on that day in the future. The ABCDE list provides as a great visual to help you organize what truly is the most important thing for you to be focusing on. Often, the C, D or E tasks may seem more enjoyable to do. I'd encourage you to be extremely honest with yourself in what is actually most important for you to achieve your grander goals in life. A regular list makes us focus on the easier tasks or things that seem more fun. With a regular list, we associate through looking at it that all of the tasks are of equal importance. Often times, there are things on those lists that are more important to get done. The ABCDE list create a great visual representation of that is truly the most important thing that you must get done. Use this tool to your advantage to maximize your time and productivity!

14

Create a reward for successes and a consequence for failures

When we were children, we would test our parents to see what we could get away with. If we displayed negative behavior or actions, our parents would often punish us. We were less likely to act in this way again or at least think twice about engaging in it. On the other end, if we achieved something or were acting in a way that we were proud of, we would be rewarded with praise or even some type of toy. Having both rewards and consequences towards our goals set a different metric where we are able to create a further incentive towards hitting our goals. This ends up being able to better rely on ourselves while saving our time and more effectively managing it.

Set consequences to not hitting a goal. We are actually more motivated to avoid pain than to seek pleasure. If we are to have $100 taken from us, we are more likely to spring into action and fight however this happened. There would at least be a strong emotional reaction to it. This is stronger than if you had the opportunity or found $100. You have a stronger reaction of losing than gaining. We can use this to our advantage to make sure we reach our goals. An example of a consequence could be that if you do not achieve your goal in 1 week, then you must go a whole week without drinking coffee if you are a daily coffee drinker. The pain or loss is felt. There are real consequences to not hitting this goal. We can use this pain of loss to better reach our goals. Perhaps you may set a consequence such as "If I don't reach this goal by the end of the week, I will donate to this charity that I like". The thing about that goal is that you may justify that it's actually a good thing if you don't reach your goal as you would be donating to a charity that you support. While the loss of giving money away is there, you can justify that it's for the greater good. I suggest to make the consequences of not reaching these goals to be doing something that you don't like. For example, if you align with a political party, make your consequence of not achieving your goal to donate to the political party which you oppose. That way you will be more motivated to not let that happen and actually achieve your goal. Other goal examples are things such as sleeping on the floor, giving up a food or activity that you enjoy or donating to charities you definitely don't support. Use your pain of loss to your advantage to achieve your goals!

Set rewards for hitting a goal. When we have something to look forward to, we are more likely to do something with some positivity. We also reinforce that goods things happen when you are to reach the goals that you set for yourself. Perhaps you have a gym and training goal. Let's say your goal is to go to the gym 3 times in a week. You set yourself a reward for this goal by going out to a nice steak dinner. If your goal is to put on muscle through weight training at the gym, this reward of the steak dinner compliments your goal of working out due to the high protein amount in a steak. Another example is to run three times a week. If you achieve this, you will buy yourself some new running pants as a reward. The more you can make these rewards compliment your goals, the more likely they are to turn into a new and positive habit.

29

15

Tell people about what you're working on

When we tell ourselves that we are going to do something, we do it with the goal that it will happen. Sometimes we fall short of these and that lowers our own trust and self-esteem. We may even come up with an elaborate story as to why we fell short of this goal. We may even forget about it completely. It is our own private thing that we can sweep under the rug. The main consequence is a bit of lost trust for ourselves. It creates a habit of not doing the things we told ourselves we were going to do. It doesn't hurt anyone but us at the end of the day.

When we tell others our goals, it becomes more real. We have spoken our goals out loud. It makes us accountable. If you tell someone what you're working towards, they hear you. They will usually ask how you're doing on the goal you told them about the next time they see you. If you didn't accomplish your goal, you either have to tell them that you didn't get it done or lie to them that you did. It's a horrible feeling either way. You start to be seen as the person that is all talk and no action. On the other hand, if they ask about your progression and you have completed it and tell them, they pay attention and will likely give you

30

praise. They start to take notice of the fact that you are an individual who does things that they say that they are going to do. You may even begin to share goals with one another and work towards them with your new accountability partner.

You may have a friend who you tell about your interest in running more. They may actually have the same thought as you. You may even schedule a time for you to both meet and run together. If you don't show up, you're not only letting yourself down but your friend also. The pain is doubled. On the positive end, you and your friend get to celebrate your wins together. Accountability can work in the form of your environment. If you are a student and need to get some school work done, it can be effective to go to the library to study. The library will often consist of a space where other students are there to accomplish similar goals who also are studying. Naturally, you're going to be quitter in this environment and do your work as everyone else is. Instead, if you went to a busy bar with games of pool and people chatting, it would be more difficult for you to focus on your school work you need to get done. Use the tools of your environment to help you in reaching your goals. This can be a very strong time saver which can then allow you more time to do the things you want to do after you do the things you know you need to be doing to reach your goal.

16

Final thoughts

Thank-you for taking the time to read this book. I hope these ideas shared and practical tips will serve you well. Time is truly our most valuable asset. You are the CEO of your own life. Nobody cares more about the outcomes of your life than you do. No one knows you better than you know yourself. You spend 24 hours a day with yourself. You know your deepest and darkest secrets. You also know your wildest hopes and dreams. You have one life. Don't count the days. Let's make the days count. You are powerful. You know exactly what you need to be doing. Don't find time. Create it.

www.ingramcontent.com/pod-product-compliance
Lightning Source LLC
Chambersburg PA
CBHW070725160726
48003CB00006BA/2380